D1461122

WANT TO BE A KNIGHT?

Paul Mason

Published 2011 by
A&C Black Publishers Ltd.
36 Soho Square, London, W1D 3QY

www.acblack.com

ISBN   HB 978-1-4081-3364-4
       PB 978-1-4081-3359-0

This book is produced using paper that is made from wood grown in managed, sustainable forests. It is natural, renewable and recyclable. The logging and manufacturing processes conform to the environmental regulations of the country of origin.

Produced for A&C Black by Calcium. www.calciumcreative.co.uk

Printed and bound in China by C&C Offset Printing Co.

All the internet addresses given in this book were correct at the time of going to press. The author and publishers regret any inconvenience caused if addresses have changed or sites have ceased to exist, but can accept no responsibility for any such changes.

Acknowledgements

The publishers would like to thank the following for their kind permission to reproduce their photographs:

Cover: Shutterstock
Pages: Dreamstime: Aliced 13, Diademimages 21, Iakov Filimonov 10, Sergey Khruschov 16, Ints Vikamanis 1, 8; Photolibrary: The British Library 20; Shutterstock: Isa Ismail 9, Litvin Leonid 5, Jose Marines 3, 6, Muránsky 17, Nichola Piccillo 14, Puchan 11, Raulin 7, 12, Topal 18, Makarova Viktoria 15, Darja Vorontsova 19, Elena Yakusheva 4.

Contents

A Knight's World 4

Born a Knight 6

Getting Started 8

Good Enough? 10

Weapons 12

Warhorses 14

Knight Rules 16

War Practice 18

Made It! 20

Glossary 22

Further Reading 23

Index 24

A Knight's World

Long ago, when knights were alive, life was not much fun for most people. There were a lot of wars, a lot of disease, and not a lot to eat.

A knight's life

It was a different story for knights – they got all the good food and lived in **castles**! So, of course, everyone wanted to be a knight.

Knights wore helmets for protection.

A tough job

Read on to find out
what it took to be
a knight – will you
still want to be one?

Helmet

Born a Knight

Only boys who come from very important and very **wealthy** families can become knights.

From father to son

Most boys become knights because their father is a knight. They have to pass many tests first, though.

Knights get to live in amazing castles. Cool!

Servant

Help on hand

Knights have lots of **servants** who look after them and their horses.

Getting Started

A boy who wants to become a knight must leave home when he is seven years old. He goes to work for a **lord**.

Sword

Is it hard work?

A **trainee** knight must do lots of different jobs for his lord. He is called a **page**.

Pages learn how to fight, too.

Toilet

This job stinks!

Pages do some truly horrid jobs (that no one else wants to do), such as cleaning the toilet. Gross!

Good Enough?

A page must be a good fighter by the time he is fourteen. If he isn't up to scratch by then, he is sent back home.

What if he makes it?
If a page does carry on with his training, he becomes a **squire**. Then he works for a knight.

Armour

 A squire's job includes cleaning lots of **armour**!

Squire

Into battle!

Life as a squire is dangerous, because he must fight with his knight in battle.

Weapons

A squire must look after his knight's armour, shields, and weapons. This is one of his most important jobs.

Why are weapons important?

A knight's life depends on all his weapons working well, so it is important that his squire takes care of them.

 Swords must be kept really, really sharp!

Flail

War tools

A knight's weapons include **lances**, swords, axes, **maces**, and **flails**. He uses them to bash, mash, and smash!

Warhorses

One of a squire's jobs is to look after his knight's warhorse. This is a really tough battle horse.

Are warhorses brave?

A warhorse is specially trained for battle, so it will still charge even if arrows are flying through the air.

 A warhorse can squash enemies into the ground.

Rich man's ride!

Keeping a warhorse costs money because they must be fed with lots of hay and oats.

Knight Rules

Knights have lots of rules about how to behave. They must stick to them carefully.

Knights must never, ever...

- Cheat or lie. No one will trust a knight who does not tell the truth.
- Run away in battle. A knight must be brave so his soldiers will follow him.

Ordinary soldiers are killed and not taken prisoner.

Caught in battle

Knights are taken prisoner in battle. A **ransom** is then paid to free them.

War Practice

Knights practise for war by fighting each other at great **tournaments**. Normally, two knights fight each other to win a prize.

Does a squire fight too?

A squire helps his knight with his armour and weapons, but he does not fight until he is a knight.

Hello, ladies!

Knights fight for more than money – they also hope to **impress** ladies!

Knights sometimes fight on foot.

Made It!

A squire is often killed in battle. But if he lives to be twenty-one, he may finally become a knight.

How is a squire made a knight?

A squire is made a knight by his king. The king touches him on his shoulders and says "Arise, Sir Knight!" From that moment on he is a knight.

A squire becomes a knight.

King

Don't relax yet

No one wants to end up as a skeleton, but if a knight doesn't die in battle he will probably die from a horrible disease.

Glossary

armour metal suit worn to protect the body in battle

castles huge stone buildings in which knights lived

flails heavy clubs with a chain and a spiked ball

impress to make someone think you are great

lances long, spear-like weapons

lord important man who had a large house or castle

maces long clubs with a heavy weight on the end

page boy training to be a knight

ransom money paid to free someone

trainee person who is learning to do a job

servants people whose job is to do whatever they are told by someone who is in charge of them

squire knight's personal servant

tournaments fights in which knights test their skills

wealthy to have a lot of money

Further Reading

Websites

Find out more about knights, including how people became a knight, at:
www.middle-ages.org.uk/steps-to-knighthood.htm

See on YouTube how knights jousted. Ask an adult to key the words 'knight, jousting' into this website and help you select a video at:
www.youtube.com

Books

Imagine You're A Knight! by Meg Clibbon, Annick Press (2005).

Medieval Knights (Fierce Fighters) by Charlotte Guillain, Raintree (2010).

The Usborne Official Knight's Handbook by Sam Taplin, Usborne (2006).

Index

armour 10, 12, 18
axes 13

battles 11, 14, 16, 17,
    20, 21

castles 4, 6

disease 4, 21

fighting 8, 10–11, 18–19
flails 13

helmets 4, 5
horses 7, 14–15

king 20
knight, becoming 20

lances 13
lord 8

maces 13

page 8–9, 10

ransom 17
rules 16–17

servants 7
shields 12
squire 10–11, 12, 14,
    18, 20
swords 8, 12, 13

tests 6
toilet 9
tournaments 18
trainee 8

warhorses 14–15
wealthy 6
weapons 12–13, 18